TAMBIKA

A Soulful GUIDE BACK TO YOU

MICHÈLE TAMBIKA

TABLE OF CONTENTS

HOW TO USE THIS GUIDE

This isn't just another wellness book filled with rules to follow. This is a heart-to-heart conversation about finding your way back to yourself when life has pulled you in every direction except the one that truly matters.

This guide is meant to be lived, not just read.

Take what resonates. Leave what doesn't. Write notes on the pages. Fold the corners of pages that speak to you. Make it messy, make it yours.

Some sections might hit you deeply today and feel irrelevant next month. That's perfect — you're evolving, and so should your relationship with these words.

There's no right way to use this guide:

- Read it all at once, or jump to whatever section calls to you
- Use it as a daily companion or a weekly check-in
- Share practices with friends or keep them sacred to yourself
- Adapt everything to fit your unique life and needs

The reflection pages are yours to fill however feels good — stream-of-consciousness writing, bullet points, drawings, or just a few words that capture how you're feeling.

Most importantly: Trust yourself. Your intuition knows what you need better than any guide ever could. I'm just here to remind you of what you already know.

Let this be a bridge back to yourself.

WELCOME HOME

You found your way here, and that's not an accident.

TAMBIKA isn't a brand or a trend or something I built to fix you. It's a space I created from my heart because I know what it feels like to lose yourself. To wake up one day and wonder where you went in all the noise, all the expectations, all the ways you tried to be everything for everyone except yourself.

I know what it's like to feel empty even when your life looks full. To smile while your soul is screaming. To have everything you thought you wanted and still feel like something is missing.

This guide isn't here to tell you what to do. You already know. Deep down, beneath all the doubt and the fear and the stories you've been told about who you should be — you know.

TAMBIKA is just here to remind you.

That healing doesn't follow rules. That your intuition is wiser than any expert. That softness is not weakness. That you are allowed to take up space, to rest, to change your mind, to choose yourself.

Take a breath. You're home now.

MY STORY
(THE REAL ONE)

I used to think healing meant having it all figured out. That there would be this moment where everything clicked and I'd never feel lost again.

But healing isn't a straight line. It's more like waves — sometimes you're riding high, feeling like you can conquer the world, and sometimes you're underwater, struggling to remember which way is up.

There were mornings I couldn't get out of bed, not because I was lazy, but because the weight of trying to be perfect was crushing me. There were nights I cried myself to sleep, feeling so disconnected from everyone around me, including myself.

The world told me to hustle harder, smile brighter, be grateful for what I had. But none of that touched the ache inside — the feeling that I was living someone else's life.

What saved me wasn't another productivity hack or positive thinking exercise. It was finally giving myself permission to feel. To stop running from the pain and start listening to what it was trying to tell me.

I started writing again — not the polished stuff I thought people wanted to read, but the messy, honest truth of what was happening inside me. I started moving my body not to look a certain way, but to feel alive again. I started cooking with intuition instead of recipes, painting when words weren't enough, acting and modeling as ways to express what was trapped inside.

Creativity became my prayer. My way back to myself.

And slowly, in moments I couldn't predict or control, I started remembering who I was underneath all the layers of who I thought I should be.

That's what TAMBIKA is — a return. Not to some perfect version of yourself, but to the truth that was always there, waiting for you to come home.

Reflection Space *What parts of my story resonate with you? What is your heart trying to tell you right now?*

_____

_____

_____

_____

_____

_____

_____

_____

_____

_____

_____

_____

_____

MORNING LIGHT

I don't believe in rigid morning routines. Life is too unpredictable, too beautiful in its messiness for that. But I do believe in rhythm — in choosing what feels right for your soul that day.

Some mornings I wake up and need to move my body, to stretch and breathe and remember I'm alive. Other mornings I need to be still, to sit with my tea and watch the world wake up around me.

Here's what has held me when everything else felt uncertain:

Gentle Movement:

Yoga, walking, stretching — especially outside where I can breathe in fresh air and feel connected to nature. Not because I have to, but because it feels good to be present in my body again. To feel into what it needs. Sometimes it's strong, powerful poses that remind me of my strength. Sometimes it's gentle, nurturing stretches that hold me like a hug.

Warm Water Ritual:

Lemon, ginger, honey — this simple combination signals to my body that I'm choosing care. The warmth in my belly, the ritual of preparation, the intentional start to my day. It's not about the health benefits (though they're there). It's about love in liquid form.

Tea as Medicine:

Each cup is chosen by how I feel, not by what I should drink. Green tea when I need clarity. Chamomile when I need softness. Ginger when I need grounding. The act of brewing, of waiting, of sitting with warmth between my hands — it's all medicine.

Breathing Into Being:

Even three minutes changes everything. I'm not trying to empty my mind or reach some enlightened state. I'm just arriving. Feeling my breath, feeling my body, feeling myself settle into this moment, this day, this life that is mine.

Skincare as Self-Love:

This isn't about looking perfect. It's about tending to myself the way I would tend to something precious. The cool water on my face, the gentle application of serums and creams — it's a daily reminder that I am worth caring for.

Morning Pages:

A few paragraphs of whatever wants to come out. No editing, no judgment, no making it pretty. Just letting my thoughts and feelings flow onto paper so they don't stay trapped inside me. Start small and let it grow naturally — some days it might be just a few sentences, other days it might flow into pages. It's like taking out the emotional trash — clearing space for what wants to come through.

Words of Power:

Not affirmations I don't believe, but truths I'm growing into. "I am worthy of Love" might feel like a lie on hard days, but "I am learning to Love myself" feels possible. Meet yourself where you are.

Sacred Stillness:

Sometimes the most radical thing you can do is nothing. In a world that demands constant doing, just being is revolutionary.

My Morning Intentions:

What does your soul need to start the day feeling nourished?

_____

_____

_____

_____

_____

_____

_____

_____

_____

_____

_____

_____

WHEN THE SUN SETS

Evenings are for release. For releasing the day and making space for rest and renewal.

Digital Sunset:

I put my phone away at least an hour before sleep. Not because I'm against technology, but because I'm for peace. I read books that feed my soul, write in my journal, or just sit in silence. I let myself remember what it feels like to be alone with my own thoughts without needing to share them with the world.

Evening Tea Ceremony:

Chamomile for calming, lavender for peace, lemon balm for releasing the day's tensions. I brew it slowly, drink it mindfully, let it remind my nervous system that it's safe to rest.

Body Gratitude:

Gentle stretches, soft movements, conscious breathing. Not to accomplish anything, just to say thank you to this body that carried me through another day. To soften what got tight, to release what got stuck.

Washing Away the Day:

My evening skincare routine is a ritual of return. Cool water washing away everything that isn't mine — the stress, the expectations, the energy of others. Gentle serums and creams soothing my skin and my spirit. I look at myself in the mirror with tenderness instead of criticism.

Journal as Release:

Not productive journaling, but emotional exhaling. What felt heavy today? What brought me joy? What do I need to let go of before I sleep? I write until I feel empty in the best way — spacious, clear, ready for dreams.

Breath as Bridge:

Long, slow inhales. Even longer, softer exhales. Sometimes with a sigh, letting sound carry out whatever I'm still holding onto. Each breath a bridge between the day that was and the rest that's coming.

Sleep Intentions:

Simple words whispered to my soul before sleep: "I release today with gratitude. I welcome deep rest. I trust tomorrow to unfold perfectly." Not magical thinking, but loving intention.

A few drops of lavender essential oil on my pillow — this simple ritual signals to my nervous system that it's time for deep restoration. Sleep isn't just recovery; it's when your soul processes the day and prepares for tomorrow.

Evening Release:

What are you ready to let go of today? What are you grateful for?

Releasing:

_____

_____

_____

Grateful for:

_____

_____

_____

_____

_____

_____

QUESTIONS FOR YOUR SOUL

When life gets loud and you can't feel yourself anymore, these questions bring me back to center:

Where am I forcing instead of flowing?

What part of me is asking to be heard right now?

Where can I choose softness over self-judgment today?

What would it feel like to be completely supported — and how can I give that to myself?

What am I ready to release that no longer serves my highest good?

If I trusted myself completely, what would I do differently?

Where am I abandoning myself to be understood by others?

What does my heart know that my mind is afraid to admit?

Use these whenever you need a moment of honest conversation with yourself. Write the answers, speak them out loud, or just hold them in your heart. Trust what comes up.

Soul Dialogue:

Choose one question that calls to you today and explore it here:

Question:

_____

_____

My truth:

_____

_____

_____

_____

_____

_____

_____

_____

_____

_____

_____

THE BREATH OF LIFE

Breath is how I come back to myself. Always.

It's free, it's simple, it's always available. When everything else feels complicated, breath is simple truth.

Box Breathing for Grounding:

Inhale for 4 counts, hold for 4, exhale for 4, hold for 4. Repeat until you feel your nervous system settle. This isn't about perfection — if you need to adjust the counts, do it. Your body knows what it needs.

Open Release Breathing:

Deep inhale through your nose, filling your belly, your ribs, your chest. Then exhale with a sound — a sigh, an "ahh," whatever wants to come out. Let the sound carry away whatever you're ready to release.

Heart-Belly Connection:

Place one hand on your heart, one on your belly. Breathe into both spaces. Feel the connection between your emotional center and your intuitive center. Sometimes I just stay here, not trying to fix anything, just feeling myself alive and present.

Breath of Gratitude:

Inhale appreciation for something in your life. Exhale any complaints or resistance. Continue until you feel your energy shift from lacking to grateful, from heavy to light.

Remember: there's no wrong way to breathe consciously. The point isn't perfect technique — it's loving presence with yourself.

WORDS THAT HEAL

Affirmations aren't magic spells. They're reminders of truths we're growing into.

I don't repeat words I don't believe. Instead, I speak the truth of where I am and where I'm going:

I am learning to trust myself completely.

I am worthy of love exactly as I am.

I choose to move through life with an open heart.

I release what no longer serves my highest good. My intuition is my most trusted guide.

I am allowed to take up space in this world.

I create from authenticity, not for approval.

I am becoming the person I've always been inside.

Love flows through me and returns to me multiplied.

I am exactly where I need to be right now.

My healing helps heal the world.

I trust the timing of my life.

Create your own. You already know what you need to hear. Write affirmations that feel true or almost true, words you can grow into. Speak them when you need reminding of who you really are.

My Personal Affirmations:

What truths is your soul ready to grow into?

_____

_____

_____

_____

_____

_____

_____

_____

_____

_____

_____

TEA AS MEDICINE

Tea is an essential part of my daily life — not just for health, but for comfort, for ritual, for the simple act of nourishing myself.

It's grounding in a world that moves too fast. It's nurturing when I need mothering. It's ceremony when I need the sacred in the ordinary.

Ginger:

For when I need warming and grounding. It aids digestion, reduces inflammation, settles nausea, but more than that — it's fire in a cup when I feel cold or disconnected.

Lemon Balm:

My nervous system's best friend. It calms anxiety, supports restful sleep, soothes emotional turbulence. When the world feels too loud, lemon balm whispers "it's okay to be soft."

Chamomile:

For releasing emotional tension held in the body. It helps with digestion and promotes rest, but I reach for it when I need to soften, when I've been holding myself too tightly.

Lavender:

Pure peace in plant form. It eases stress and encourages inner stillness. When my mind won't stop spinning, lavender reminds me that calm is my birthright.

Peppermint:

For mental clarity and cooling inflammation. It supports digestion and clears the mind. I drink it when I need to cut through confusion and find my center.

Green Tea:

When I need gentle energy and focus. The ritual of preparing it, the earthy taste, the sustained energy without jitters — it's mindfulness you can drink.

These plants are teachers. They've inspired a future vision for TAM-BIKA tea blends — because I believe healing can be warm, slow, and steeped in nature's wisdom.

My Tea Ritual:

What does your perfect tea moment look like? How do you want to feel?

_____

_____

_____

_____

_____

_____

GROUNDING WHEN THE WORLD FEELS TOO MUCH

When anxiety rises, when I feel scattered or disconnected from myself, these practices bring me back to earth:

Barefoot on Sacred Ground:

Step outside, remove your shoes, feel the earth beneath your feet and breathe in the fresh air. Grass, soil, sand — it doesn't matter. Let the earth and fresh air remind you who you are. Feel yourself held by something bigger than your worries.

The Heart-Belly Bridge:

Place one hand on your heart, one on your belly. This connects your emotional wisdom with your intuitive knowing. Breathe into both spaces and listen to what they're telling you.

Three-Minute Belly Breathing:

Let your breath drop into your lower belly, expanding it like a balloon. Each exhale releases something you don't need to carry. Continue until you feel yourself settle.

Warm Mug Meditation:

Hold a warm cup of tea or water with both hands. Feel the warmth transfer from the mug to your palms. Let this simple warmth achor you in the present moment. Sometimes the smallest comforts are the most profound.

Gratitude as Grounding:

Name three things you're grateful for right now. They can be huge or tiny — the Sun on your face, the roof over your head, the breath in your lungs. Gratitude shifts your energy from lack to abundance without forcing positivity.

Body Scan with Love:

Starting at the top of your head, slowly scan down through your body. Notice where you're holding tension and breathe Love into those places. This isn't about fixing anything — it's about loving yourself as you are.

CREATIVITY AS PRAYER

I create to survive. I create to thrive. I create because something inside me demands expression.

Painting when words aren't enough. Writing when I need to understand what I'm feeling. Cooking from intuition instead of recipes. Moving my body like dance, like worship, like celebration.

Modeling and acting became ways to explore different parts of myself, to give voice to emotions that needed to be seen and felt. Every creative act is a conversation between my soul and the world.

You don't need to be an "artist" to be creative. You just need to let something move through you.

Creative Healing Practices:

Write morning pages — a few paragraphs of stream-of-consciousness writing. No editing, no judgment, just letting whatever wants to come out flow onto paper. Start with what feels manageable and let it grow naturally.

Move without choreography — put on music and let your body move however it wants. This isn't about looking good; it's about feeling alive.

Cook intuitively — choose ingredients based on what your body is craving, not what a recipe tells you. Let cooking become a meditation.

Photograph beauty — capture moments that make you feel something. Light through windows, hands holding tea, shadows on walls, flowers in nature, the sky at different times of day. Train your eye to see magic in the ordinary.

Create color — whether it's painting, coloring, or just playing with makeup. Let color express what words cannot.

The point isn't to create something perfect. It's to give your inner world a way to communicate with the outer world. It's to remember that you are not just a consumer of beauty — you are a creator of it.

Creative Expression *What wants to be created through you? How does your soul long to express itself?*

_____

_____

_____

_____

_____

_____

_____

_____

_____

_____

_____

_____

THE DARK DAYS
(AND WHY THEY MATTER)

I need to tell you something: the dark days are not your enemy.

I know it doesn't feel that way when you're in them. When everything feels heavy and nothing makes sense and you can't remember why you used to feel hopeful about anything.

But those days — the ones where you can barely get out of bed, where your heart feels so heavy, where you wonder if you're broken beyond repair — those days are doing something important.

They're composting your old self. Breaking down what no longer serves you so something new can grow.

When the darkness comes:

Let yourself feel it. Don't rush to fix it or think your way out of it or paste a smile over it. Darkness requires darkness. Some things can only be processed in the deep, quiet places of the soul.

Rest more than feels reasonable. Your body and spirit are doing invisible work. Honor that with extra gentleness.

Cry when you need to cry. Tears are not weakness — they're release. They're your soul cleaning house.

Reach out, but only to safe people. The ones who can sit with you in the darkness without trying to turn on all the lights.

Trust that this is temporary, even when it doesn't feel that way. The Sun always comes back. Always.

Remember: You're not falling apart. You're falling together. Sometimes we have to dissolve before we can reconstitute into who we're becoming.

Dark day survival kit:

- Warm baths with Epsom salts
- Gentle music that matches your mood
- Nourishing food that comforts your soul - choose healthy options that make you feel good.
- Journal pages for the messy feelings
- Nature, even if it's just a houseplant
- Early bedtimes
- Permission to do nothing productive
- Reminders that this feeling is temporary

The darkness is not punishment. It's transformation. Trust the process, even when you can't see where it's leading.

Honoring the Darkness *What is this difficult time trying to teach you? What wants to be released?*

_____

_____

_____

_____

_____

BOUNDARIES ARE SELF-LOVE

Learning to set boundaries was learning to love myself.

For so long, I thought love meant saying yes to everything, being available to everyone, making myself small so others could be comfortable. I thought boundaries were selfish, mean, unloving.

But boundaries aren't walls to keep people out. They're gates that protect what's sacred while still allowing love to flow.

What boundaries look like in practice:

Saying no without explaining why when something doesn't align with your values or energy.

Choosing not to engage with people who consistently drain or disrespect you.

Protecting your time and energy like the precious resources they are. Speaking your truth even when others might not like it.

Leaving situations that consistently make you feel bad about yourself. Not absorbing other people's emotions as if they were your own. Asking for what you need instead of hoping others will guess.

How to set boundaries without guilt:

Remember that you're not responsible for other people's reactions to your boundaries. You're only responsible for setting them with love and clarity.

Practice the phrase: "That doesn't work for me." You don't owe anyone a detailed explanation.

Notice that people who truly love you will respect your boundaries, even if they don't understand them.

Start small. Set one small boundary today and notice that the world doesn't end.

Remember that every time you honor your own needs, you're teaching others how to treat you.

Boundaries aren't about being difficult. They're about being authentic. They're about honoring the truth of who you are and what you need to thrive.

The people who are meant to be in your life will appreciate your boundaries because they want you to be healthy and whole.

My Boundary Practice *Where in your life do you need stronger boundaries? What would that look like?*

_____

_____

_____

_____

_____

THE HEALING POWER
OF SOLITUDE

Some of my most profound healing has happened in solitude — not because I was avoiding people, but because I was finally spending time with the most important person in my life: me.

In our hyperconnected world, solitude has become almost counter-cultural. We're afraid of being alone with our thoughts, afraid of what we might discover in the silence.

But solitude is where you remember who you are underneath all the roles you play for others.

What solitude has taught me:

My own company is actually quite enjoyable when I stop judging my-self.

The answers I'm seeking aren't in other people's opinions — they're in the quiet voice that comes through when everything else gets still.

I don't need constant stimulation to feel okay. In fact, I need the oppo-site — space to just be.

My intuition speaks most clearly when I'm not drowning it out with external noise.

Self-love isn't selfish — it's essential. You can't give from an empty cup.

How to practice sacred solitude:

Turn off all devices for a set period of time. Start with 30 minutes if an hour feels too scary. Increase your time offline the more you get used to it and watch how beautiful life gets.

Take yourself on dates. Go to a museum, a cafe, a park. Enjoy your own company.

Eat meals in silence sometimes, really tasting your food instead of scrolling while you eat.

Sit in nature without agenda. Don't try to meditate or process or figure anything out. Just be present with the trees, the sky, the earth. Listen to the birds, the wind, the natural sounds around you.

Journal without censoring yourself. Let whatever wants to come out onto the page.

Take baths without rushing. Light candles, add essential oils, let yourself luxuriate in your own care.

The difference between loneliness and solitude:

Loneliness is the feeling that something is missing. Solitude is the feeling that nothing is missing — that you are complete exactly as you are, right now, in this moment.

In solitude, you're not avoiding connection — you're connecting with the deepest part of yourself. And from that place of inner fullness, all your external relationships become richer.

Sacred Solitude *How can you create more meaningful alone time? What do you discover about yourself in silence?*

_____

_____

_____

_____

_____

_____

_____

_____

_____

_____

ENERGY IS EVERYTHING

I used to think I was just sensitive. That I absorbed everyone else's moods because I was empathetic. That I felt drained after being around certain people because I cared too much.

But what I've learned is that I'm an energetic being having a human experience, and energy management is just as important as time management.

Signs you're absorbing energy that isn't yours:

You feel amazing alone but drained around certain people.

You pick up the emotions of rooms you walk into.

You feel responsible for other people's feelings.

You can sense when someone is upset even when they say they're fine.

You need a lot of recovery time after social interactions.

How to protect your energy:

Before entering any space, visualize yourself surrounded by protective light. I imagine golden light around my entire body, allowing love in but keeping negativity out.

Notice how different people make you feel. Spend more time with people who energize you and less time with people who drain you.

After spending time with draining people or in heavy environments, consciously release their energy. I imagine any energy that isn't mine flowing out of my body and back to where it belongs.

Set energetic boundaries. Just because you can feel someone's pain doesn't mean you have to carry it.

Ground yourself regularly. Bare feet on earth, hands in soil, time in nature — these practices help discharge energy that isn't yours.

Clear your space. Burn sage, palo santo, or incense. Open windows. Play uplifting music. Keep your environment energetically clean.

Remember:

You are not responsible for fixing other people's energy.

It's okay to limit your time with people who consistently drain you, even if you love them.

Protecting your energy isn't selfish — it's necessary for your wellbeing and for your ability to show up authentically for others.

Your energy is sacred. Treat it that way.

Energy Awareness *Who and what energizes you? Who and what drains you? How can you honor this knowledge?*

Energizes me:

_____

_____

_____

_____

Drains me:

_____

_____

_____

_____

I will honor this by:

_____

_____

_____

_____

_____

_____

MANIFESTATION WITHOUT THE BULLSHIT

I believe in the power of intention, but I don't believe in toxic positivity or magical thinking.

Real manifestation isn't about pretending everything is perfect or forcing yourself to think positive thoughts when your world is falling apart.

Real manifestation is about aligning your inner world with your deepest values and then taking inspired action from that place of alignment.

What actually works:

Get clear on what you want and why you want it. Make sure your desires are coming from your authentic self, not from what you think you should want.

Feel into the energy of already having what you desire. Not to trick the universe, but to become the person who would naturally attract those experiences.

Take aligned action. Manifestation without action is just daydreaming. But action without alignment is just struggle.

Release attachment to specific outcomes. Trust that what's meant for you will find you, and what's not meant for you is redirecting you toward something better.

Address your inner blocks. If you're sabotaging yourself, visualizing success won't help. You need to heal the parts of you that don't believe you deserve good things.

What doesn't work:

Pretending to be positive when you're actually in pain.

Trying to manifest from ego instead of soul.

Forcing timelines that aren't natural.

Ignoring practical steps because you're waiting for magic.

Thinking you can control outcomes through pure determination alone.

The real magic:

When you align with your authentic self and trust the process, life starts flowing in ways that feel effortless. Not because you've hacked some cosmic code, but because you're finally swimming with the current instead of against it.

You start attracting people and opportunities that match your energy. You make decisions from clarity instead of fear. You take action from inspiration instead of desperation.

That's not magic — that's alignment. And it's available to you right now.

Aligned Manifestation *What do you truly desire? What actions can you take from alignment, not desperation?*

My authentic desires:

_____

_____

_____

_____

Aligned actions I can take:

_____

_____

_____

_____

_____

_____

_____

_____

FOOD AS MEDICINE, COOKING AS LOVE

The way we feed ourselves is how we love ourselves.

I stopped following diet culture and started following my intuition. Instead of eating what I thought I should eat, I began eating what made my body feel alive and nourished.

Intuitive nourishment:

Listen to your body's cravings. They're often telling you what nutrients you need.

Eat when you're hungry, stop when you're satisfied. This sounds simple but it's revolutionary in a culture that tells us to ignore our body's signals.

Choose foods that make you feel energized rather than sluggish. Notice how different foods affect your mood, energy, and mental clarity.

Cook with love and intention. The energy you put into preparing food becomes part of the food itself.

Eat without distractions sometimes. Taste your food, appreciate the colors and textures, be present with the nourishment you're giving yourself.

My nourishing essentials:

Warm lemon ginger water first thing in the morning to wake up my digestive system.

Lots of vegetables in all colors — I eat the rainbow because different colors provide different nutrients. I choose organic and local when possible.

Healthy fats that make my brain happy — avocados, nuts, olive oil. Always the highest quality I can find.

Protein that keeps me stable — organic eggs, legumes, quinoa, grass-fed beef, free-range chicken, whatever feels good and comes from good sources.

Herbal teas throughout the day for different needs — energy, calm, digestion, comfort.

Quality matters: I prioritize high-quality, organic ingredients whenever possible. When it comes to animal products, I choose grass-fed, free-range, and ethically sourced options. Your body deserves the best fuel, and you can truly feel the difference when you nourish yourself with high-quality, whole foods.

Cooking as self-care:

I cook without recipes sometimes, just combining ingredients that call to me. This is meditation, creativity, and nourishment all at once.

I prepare meals like I'm feeding someone I love deeply — because I am.

I keep my kitchen stocked with ingredients that make me happy, so nourishing myself is always possible.

Remember: there's no perfect way to eat. There's only the way that makes you feel most alive and healthy. Trust your body — it knows what it needs.

MOVEMENT AS MEDICINE

I move my body not to punish it for what it ate or to force it into a certain shape, but to celebrate what it can do and to feel alive in my own skin.

Why I move:

To release emotions that get stuck in my body.

To feel strong and capable.

To connect with my physical self in a loving way.

To boost my energy and mood naturally.

To practice being present in my body.

How I move:

Yoga - My non-negotiable. It's moving meditation, strength building, flexibility training, and therapy all in one. Every pose is a conversation with my body about what it needs today.

Walking - Simple, accessible, grounding. I walk to think, to process emotions, to breathe fresh air, to feel my feet on the earth.

Dancing - Free-form movement to music that makes me feel alive. This isn't about looking good - it's about feeling good.

Stretching - Gentle, intuitive stretching throughout the day to release tension and stay connected to my body.

Swimming — When available, there's something about being held by water that feels like healing.

The most important thing:

Move in ways that feel good to you. Ignore what everyone else is doing. Your body is unique, your needs are unique, your joy is unique. Some days you might want to sweat and push your limits. Other days you might want gentle, restorative movement. Both are perfect.

Listen to your body. It will tell you what it needs if you pay attention. Exercise shouldn't be punishment. It should be celebration — celebration of this amazing body that carries you through life.

My Movement Practice *How does your body like to move? What makes you feel most alive and connected?*

_____

_____

_____

_____

_____

_____

_____

_____

THE ART OF RECEIVING

I had to learn how to receive love, compliments, help, and abundance. For years, I deflected good things because I didn't feel worthy of them.

But receiving is just as important as giving. When you refuse to receive, you deny others the joy of giving to you.

Learning to receive:

When someone compliments you, say "thank you" instead of deflecting or explaining why they're wrong.

Ask for help when you need it. Independence is beautiful, but so is interdependence.

Allow people to do nice things for you without feeling guilty or obligated to return the favor immediately.

Notice when good things happen to you instead of only focusing on problems.

Accept opportunities that come your way, even if you don't feel 100% ready.

Blocks to receiving:

Feeling unworthy of good things.

Believing you have to earn love and kindness.

Thinking that needing help makes you weak. Feeling guilty when life goes well for you.

Trying to control everything instead of allowing life to flow.

The practice:

Start small. Let someone buy you coffee. Accept a genuine compliment. Allow a friend to help you with something.

Notice your internal resistance to receiving and breathe through it.

Practice gratitude for what you already have. Appreciation opens you to receiving more.

Remember that your worthiness isn't earned — it's inherent. You deserve good things simply because you exist.

When you become a good receiver, you become a better giver. You understand the joy of generosity because you've experienced the grace of receiving.

Opening to Receive

What are you ready to receive more of? Where do you notice resistance to receiving?

Ready to receive: _____

I notice resistance when:

_____

_____

_____

_____

TRUST AND SURRENDER

The most difficult and most liberating lesson I've learned is how to trust the process of life.

For so long, I tried to control outcomes, force timelines, make things happen through pure determination. I exhausted myself trying to be the director of a movie where I was only meant to be the star.

What trust looks like:

Taking aligned action and then releasing attachment to specific results.

Believing that life is working for you, not against you, even when you can't see the bigger picture.

Staying open to possibilities you haven't even imagined yet.

Making decisions from inner knowing rather than external pressure.

Being willing to change direction when something isn't working, instead of forcing it because you invested time or energy.

What surrender doesn't mean:

Giving up or being passive.

Accepting situations that are genuinely harmful.

Ignoring your intuition or not advocating for yourself.

Letting others make decisions for you.

What surrender does mean:

Doing your part and letting life do its part.

Being flexible about how things unfold while staying committed to your values.

Trusting that delays and redirections are often protection or preparation.

Allowing things to be easier than you think they have to be.

The practice:

When you're trying to force something, pause and ask: "How can I let this be easier?"

Notice when you're swimming upstream and see if there's a current you can ride instead.

Practice the phrase: "This or something better."

Remember that you can't control other people, circumstances, or timelines - but you can control your response to all of those things.

Trust isn't blind faith. Trust is knowing that you can handle whatever comes, and that life is always giving you exactly what you need for your growth and evolution.

Practicing Surrender *Where in your life are you trying to force outcomes? How can you surrender while still taking aligned action?*

I'm forcing:

_____

_____

_____

_____

I can surrender by:

_____

_____

_____

_____

Aligned actions I can take:

_____

_____

_____

_____

_____

SIGNS YOU'RE HEALING

Healing isn't linear, and it doesn't look like social media posts of people jumping for joy on mountaintops. Real healing is quiet, subtle, and often happens in moments you don't even notice.

You're healing when:

You start choosing yourself without guilt.

You can sit in silence without needing to fill it with noise or activity.

You feel your emotions without being overwhelmed by them.

You set boundaries and don't immediately want to apologize for them.

You stop seeking validation from people who can't see your worth.

You choose rest without feeling lazy.

You speak your truth even when your voice shakes.

You can be happy for others without comparing their journey to yours.

You trust your intuition more than other people's opinions.

You see challenges as opportunities for growth instead of evidence that you're broken.

You love yourself on the days when you don't feel loveable.

You take care of your body as an act of love, not punishment.

You create because it brings you joy, not because you need external validation.

You can hold space for others without losing yourself in their problems.

You believe you deserve good things and don't sabotage them when they come.

Remember:

Healing isn't about becoming perfect. It's about becoming whole.

You don't heal once and then you're done. Healing is an ongoing practice of choosing Love over fear, truth over comfort, growth over stagnation.

Every small act of self-love is healing. Every boundary you set is healing. Every time you choose authenticity over acceptance, you heal a little more.

You're not broken and you don't need fixing. You're a human being having a human experience, and part of that experience is learning to love yourself unconditionally.

Celebrating My Healing *Which signs of healing do you recognize in yourself? What growth are you proud of?*

_____

_____

_____

_____

_____

A LOVE LETTER TO
YOUR FUTURE SELF

Dear Beautiful Soul Who Is Still Becoming,

I see you there, reading these words, wondering if you have what it takes to heal, to grow, to become who you know you're meant to be. You do.

I see you doubting whether you're worthy of the Love and abundance you crave.

You are.

I see you feeling alone in your struggles, like no one understands the specific way your heart breaks and mends and breaks again.

You're not alone.

Your path doesn't have to look like anyone else's. Your healing doesn't have to follow a timeline. Your growth doesn't have to be linear.

All you have to do is keep choosing Love. Love for yourself, Love for your journey, Love for the messy, beautiful, transformative process of being human.

Keep choosing truth over comfort. Keep choosing authenticity over acceptance. Keep choosing yourself even when it feels scary.

Trust that everything that has brought you to this moment – the pain, the joy, the confusion, the clarity — all of it has been necessary.

All of it has been preparing you for what's coming next.

You are not behind. You are not broken. You are not too much or not enough.

You are exactly where you need to be, learning exactly what you need to learn, becoming exactly who you're meant to become.

The world needs your specific magic. The world needs your particular way of seeing, of creating, of loving.

Don't dim your light to make others comfortable. Don't make yourself small to fit into spaces that weren't designed for your expansiveness.

You belong here. Your voice matters. Your dreams are valid.

Keep going, beautiful soul. Keep growing. Keep glowing.

The Sun is always shining, even when you can't see it through the clouds.

With infinite Love and belief in your becoming,
Your Present Self Who Knows Your Worth

Letter to Myself: *Write your own Love letter to your future self. What do you want your future self to know?*

Dear Future Me,

_____

_____

_____

_____

_____

_____

_____

_____

_____

_____

_____

_____

_____

_____

_____

_____

_____

_____

_____

_____

_____

_____

With Love, Your Present Self

SACRED RITUALS FOR DAILY DEVOTION

This isn't about perfection or checking boxes. It's about creating small, sacred moments throughout your day that remind you of who you are and what matters.

Morning Sacred Moments:

Light a candle while you drink your morning tea. Let the flame remind you that you carry light within you.

Write three things you're grateful for before you check your phone. Start your day with appreciation instead of information overload.

Set an intention for the day. Not a goal to accomplish, but a way you want to feel or show up in the world.

Look at yourself in the mirror and say something kind. Start with "Good morning, beautiful" and work up to deeper affirmations.

Take five conscious breaths before you leave your space. Arrive in your day instead of rushing into it.

Throughout the Day:

Pause between activities. Take one breath before starting something new.

Eat one meal mindfully, taking time to taste every bite without distraction.

Send a loving text to someone who matters to you.

Notice something beautiful that you usually overlook.

Ask yourself: "What do I need right now?" and then give it to yourself if possible.

Evening Sacred Moments:

Light incense or a candle to mark the transition from day to night.

Write down one thing that challenged you today and one thing that brought you joy.

Place your hands on your heart and thank your body for carrying you through another day.

Forgive yourself for anything you wish you'd done differently.

Set an intention for your sleep and dreams.

Weekly Rituals:

Take yourself on a solo date. Coffee, bookstore, park, museum-anywhere that feeds your soul.

Have a phone-free meal with someone you love.

Spend time in nature without agenda. Just be present with the earth, breathe in the fresh air, and listen to nature's sounds.

Clean and organize your space as an act of self-love.

Write a letter to your future self about what you're learning and how you're growing.

Monthly Rituals:

Review your journal entries from the past month. Notice patterns, growth, recurring themes.

Do something that scares you a little bit in service of your dreams.

Declutter something in your life - physical items, digital files, relationships, commitments.

Celebrate yourself for how far you've come, even if you're not where you want to be yet.

Plan something to look forward to in the coming month.

Remember: these are suggestions, not rules. Choose what resonates, modify what doesn't, create your own. The point is to weave sacredness into the ordinary moments of life.

My Sacred Rituals *Which rituals call to you? What sacred moments do you want to create?*

Daily:

_____

_____

_____

Weekly:

_____

_____

_____

Monthly:

_____

_____

_____

_____

THE TAMBIKA WAY

This isn't a set of rules to follow. It's a way of being that honors the truth of who you are.

We believe in:

Softness without weakness. There is incredible strength in gentleness, in vulnerability, in allowing yourself to feel deeply.

Healing that happens in spirals, not straight lines. Growth isn't linear, and neither is recovery. You might revisit the same lessons at deeper levels.

Intuition as the highest intelligence. Your inner knowing is more reliable than any external authority.

Creativity as a spiritual practice. Every act of creation is a conversation between your soul and the divine.

Rest as a radical act. In a culture that glorifies busyness, choosing rest is choosing revolution.

Boundaries as love in action. Protecting your energy and honoring your needs isn't selfish — it's sacred.

We practice:

Speaking truth even when our voice shakes.

Choosing Love over fear, even when fear feels safer.

Honoring our bodies as temples, not projects to fix.

Creating beauty wherever we go.

Supporting others in their becoming without competing or comparing.

Being authentic even when it's inconvenient for others.

We remember:

You are not broken and you don't need fixing.

Your worth is not determined by your productivity or achievements.

It's okay to outgrow people, places, and versions of yourself.

You can start over as many times as you need to.

Your sensitivity is a superpower, not a weakness.

You don't owe anyone your small self to make them comfortable.

The TAMBIKA promise:

This is a sanctuary for truth, not trends. A space for real healing, not performative wellness. A place where you can be honest about your struggles and celebrated for your growth.

You don't have to have it all figured out to belong here. You just have to be willing to keep becoming.

TOOLS FOR THE JOURNEY

When you're overwhelmed:

- Three deep breaths
- Feet on the ground
- Hand on heart
- "I am safe in this moment"

When you doubt yourself:

- List three things you've overcome
- Remember a time you trusted yourself and it worked out
- Ask: "What would I do if I truly believed in myself?"

When you feel lost:

- Get still and listen
- Write stream-of-consciousness for 10 minutes
- Go outside, breathe fresh air, listen to nature, and let it remind you who you are

When you need courage:

- Remember that courage isn't the absence of fear - it's feeling the fear and moving forward anyway
- Take one small step toward what scares you

- Surround yourself with stories of people who've done what you're trying to do

When you're lonely:

- Spend time with yourself doing something you love
- Reach out to one person who truly sees you
- Remember that feeling lonely doesn't mean you're alone

When you need to let go:

- Write what you need to release on paper and burn it safely
- Take a bath and imagine washing away what no longer serves you
- Forgive yourself for holding on longer than you needed to

When you need hope:

- Look for one small sign that things are shifting
- Remember that the darkest hour is just before dawn
- Trust that everything is working out for your highest good

A COLLECTION OF
HEALING MANTRAS

Use these when you need words to guide you back to yourself:

I am learning to trust the wisdom of my own heart.

Every breath is a new beginning.

I choose to see challenges as opportunities for growth.

My sensitivity is my strength.

I am worthy of love exactly as I am.

I release what no longer serves my highest good.

I trust the timing of my life.

I am exactly where I need to be.

My healing helps heal the world.

I choose Love over fear.

I am becoming who I've always been.

All is well in my world.

I am safe to be myself.

My dreams are valid and achievable.

I attract what I am, not what I want.

I am the author of my own story.

Peace is my natural state.

I choose joy wherever possible.

My intuition is my most trusted guide.

I am grateful for this beautiful, meaningful life.

CREATING YOUR OWN
TAMBIKA PRACTICE

The most important thing I can tell you is this: there is no right way to do this work. There is only your way.

To create your own practice:

Start where you are. Don't wait until you have the perfect setup or the right amount of time. Use what you have, start where you are, do what you can.

Choose what resonates. If something in this guide doesn't feel aligned with who you are, leave it. Take what serves you and let the rest go.

Be consistent, not perfect. It's better to do one small thing every day than to do everything perfectly once a week.

Listen to your inner wisdom. Your soul knows what it needs. Trust that knowing above any external guidance.

Allow it to evolve. Your practice will change as you change. What serves you today might not serve you next month, and that's perfect.

Make it yours. Add your own rituals, create your own affirmations, find your own ways of connecting with yourself and the sacred.

Sample daily practice (modify as needed):

Morning (10-15 minutes):

- Three conscious breaths upon waking up
- Gratitude for something in your life
- Intention setting for the day
- Warm lemon water or tea
- Brief journaling or affirmations

Midday (10-15 minutes):

- Mindful eating for one meal
- Brief nature connection (even if it's looking at the sky)
- Check in with yourself: "What do I need right now?"

Evening (10-15 minutes):

- Release the day through breath or movement
- Gratitude for three things from the day
- Brief journaling or reflection
- Gentle self-care ritual
- Setting intention for rest

Remember: This is about connection, not perfection. As you're building these habits, some days you'll do everything, some days you'll do nothing, and both are okay. The goal is to gradually weave more consciousness and self-love into your daily life until it becomes natural.

Designing My Practice *What would your ideal daily practice look like? Start small and build from there.*

Morning:

_____

_____

_____

_____

Midday:

_____

_____

_____

_____

Evening:

_____

_____

_____

_____

What I commit to starting with:

_____

_____

_____

_____

_____

THE RIPPLE EFFECT

When you heal yourself, you heal the world.

Not in some abstract, mystical way (though maybe that too), but in very real, practical ways.

When you learn to love yourself, you model self-love for everyone around you.

When you set boundaries, you give others permission to do the same.

When you choose authenticity over acceptance, you make it safer for others to be real.

When you follow your intuition, you inspire others to trust their own inner knowing.

When you pursue your dreams, you show others that dreams are meant to be lived, not just wished for.

Your healing journey matters — not just to you, but to your family, your friends, your community, and even to strangers who might be watching you from afar, wondering if it's possible to change, to grow, to become who they're meant to be.

You are not healing in isolation. You are part of a web of connection that extends far beyond what you can see.

Every time you choose Love over fear, you make it easier for someone else to do the same.

Every time you honor your truth, you give someone else permission to honor theirs.

Every time you treat yourself with kindness, you raise the standard for how love looks in this world.

This is the ripple effect of healing — it spreads outward in ways you might never know about, but that matter more than you can imagine. So keep going. Keep growing. Keep becoming.

Not just for yourself, but for all of us who need to see that transformation is possible, that healing is real, that it's never too late to become who you've always been inside.

UNTIL WE MEET AGAIN

This isn't the end — it's the beginning.

The beginning of you trusting yourself more deeply. The beginning of you honoring your needs without apology. The beginning of you creating a life that feels as good on the inside as it looks on the outside.

TAMBIKA will continue to evolve because you will continue to evolve. This guide is just one expression of a way of being that honors the sacred in the everyday, the healing in the broken places, the beauty in the becoming.

Take what serves you from these pages. Leave what doesn't. Add what's missing. Make it yours.

Remember that healing isn't a destination — it's a way of traveling. It's choosing Love over fear, truth over comfort, growth over stagnation, again and again and again.

Some days will be easier than others. Some days you'll feel like you've got it all figured out, and other days you'll wonder if you know anything at all.

Both days are perfect. Both days are part of the journey.

Trust the process. Trust yourself. Trust that everything is working out exactly as it should, even when you can't see the bigger picture.

You are not alone in this. You are surrounded by love, even when you can't feel it. You are supported by energies seen and unseen. You are exactly where you need to be.

Thank you for being here. Thank you for being you. Thank you for having the courage to grow, to heal, to become.

The world needs your light. Don't let anyone convince you to dim it.

I'll see you in the next breath, the next cup of tea, the next quiet moment when you remember who you really are.

Until then, keep shining.

With all my Love,

Michèle

ABOUT MICHÈLE

Hi beautiful soul, I'm Michèle Tambika — the heart and hands behind TAMBIKA.

My journey has been all about finding balance in a world that often feels chaotic, discovering self-care as a radical act of love, and learning to live with deep intention in every moment.

I believe that when you truly nourish your body, mind, and soul, you unlock your highest potential — and that's exactly what I want to share with you through this work.

I've always been drawn to movement and mindfulness, which is why yoga, pilates, hiking, and tennis are such essential parts of my life. Being outdoors fuels my soul, and traveling has allowed me to expand my perspective and embrace new ways of being. Meditation keeps me grounded when life gets loud, while healthy food and intuitive nutrition are at the heart of my lifestyle — I love creating my own recipes because food isn't just fuel, it's an act of self-care and creativity.

Born and raised in Switzerland, I spent five transformative years in California, where I pursued my Bachelor of Fine Arts in Acting for Film. Creativity has always been part of who I am — whether through painting, writing, photography, acting, modeling, or real estate, which became an unexpected passion when I earned my license at 23.

But beyond all the doing, at my core, I am a creator, a dreamer, and an encourager. My mission through TAMBIKA is to support others in remembering who they really are underneath all the noise — to become the most authentic, loving, powerful version of themselves.

I truly believe that with the right mindset, aligned action, and a whole lot of self-love, you can create anything your heart desires.

This guide was born from my own journey back to myself — through dark nights and bright mornings, through creativity and healing, through learning to trust my own voice above all others.

I'm so grateful you're here, and I'm honored to be part of your journey.

Let's grow, evolve, and thrive — together.

Connect with me:

Website: www.tambika.com

Follow the journey: @tambika.official

REFLECTION PAGES

What Called to Me in This Guide:

_____

_____

_____

_____

_____

_____

_____

_____

_____

_____

_____

_____

_____

_____

_____

_____

_____

_____

_____

Practices I Want to Try:

_____

_____

_____

_____

_____

_____

_____

_____

_____

_____

_____

My Biggest Insights:

_____

_____

_____

_____

_____

_____

_____

_____

_____

_____

How I Want to Feel:

_____

_____

_____

_____

_____

_____

_____

_____

_____

_____

Letters to Myself:

_____

_____

_____

_____

_____

_____

_____

_____

_____

_____

Free Flow Thoughts & Feelings:

_____

_____

_____

_____

_____

_____

_____

_____

_____

_____

Gratitude & Appreciation:

_____

_____

_____

_____

_____

_____

_____

_____

_____

_____

_____

_____

_____

_____

_____

_____

_____

Dreams & Visions:

_____

_____

_____

_____

_____

_____

_____

_____

_____

_____

_____

_____

_____

_____

_____

_____

My Healing Journey:

_____

_____

_____

_____

_____

_____

_____

_____

_____

_____

_____

_____

_____

_____

_____

What I'm Learning About Myself:

_____

_____

_____

_____

_____

Monthly Reflections:

_____

_____

_____

_____

_____

_____

_____

_____

Seasonal Check-Ins:

_____

_____

_____

_____

_____

_____

_____

_____

_____

_____

_____

_____

_____

_____

Creative Expressions:

Sacred Space for Whatever Wants to Flow:

Remember: You are everything. The world is yours.

You got this.

www.ingramcontent.com/pod-product-compliance
Lightning Source LLC
Chambersburg PA
CBHW051642120626
46551CB00015B/2185